CONTENTS

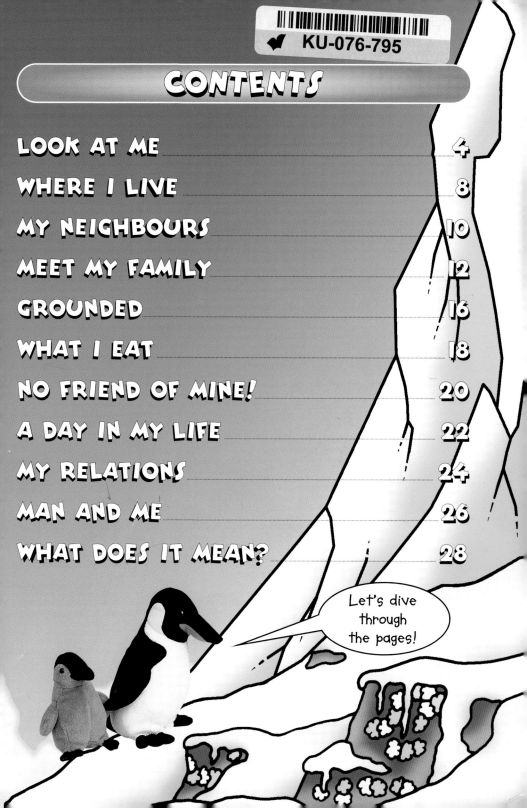

Let's dive through the pages!

LOOK AT ME

Penguins are seabirds. Unlike most birds, they cannot fly. Instead, penguins are built for swimming. A penguin has a smooth, streamlined body with wings shaped like paddles. The penguin beats its wings up and down to 'fly' through the water and uses its webbed feet and small tail to steer. Emperor penguins are the biggest penguins in the world.

DID YOU KNOW?

FINE FEATHERS

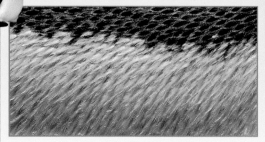

- Penguins have short, stiff feathers with tufts of down at the base. The feathers overlap, so they trap lots of air. This helps to keep penguins warm and dry.
- Penguins' feathers are more closely packed together than the feathers of most other birds. Penguins have as many as 15 feathers on a space no larger than this square:
- When a penguin is hot, it ruffles its feathers and holds its wings out from its sides to cool down.

EMPEROR PENGUIN FACTS

LATIN NAME: Aptenodytes forsteri
ANIMAL GROUP: Aves (birds)
ANIMAL FAMILY: Spheniscidae (penguins)
COLOUR: black back and head with yellow markings and a white front
SIZE: up to 1.2 m tall
WEIGHT: 20–40 kg
SPEED: swims at up to 14 km/h; walks at up to 2.8 km/h
EATS: fish, squid and shellfish
DRINKS: sea water
LIVES: up to 25 years

MY ANIMAL KINGDOM

PENGUINS

Brown Watson

ENGLAND

Dear Friend,

Welcome to My Animal Kingdom!

My name's Perry and I'm an emperor penguin.
I'm here, together with my young daughter
Priscilla, to introduce you to our wonderful icy
world. You're going to find out all about
where we live, what we eat and how we
stay warm in our freezing home.

Join us as we 'toboggan' down icy slopes or
dive through the waves to catch a fishy
dinner. There are lots of penguin facts
to discover, and you'll have great fun
meeting my family and friends.

I hope you have a terrific time as you slip and
slide your way through this book!

Perry

Come with us for a slide on the ice!

My oily feathers are waterproof.

My flipper-shaped wings are great for swimming.

My smooth, seal-like shape helps me to glide easily through the water.

A thick layer of fat under my skin keeps me warm in my icy home.

I use my tail and feet to help me to turn when I swim.

On land, I stand upright on my feet. I walk slowly over the ice.

Penguins can live both on land and in the sea. They can see very well under water, but are short-sighted on land. Penguins can hear well, too. They keep in touch with a series of different calls. A penguin also uses the position of its head, beak and body to send messages to other penguins.

My ears are tiny holes on each side of my head, but I can hear well.

I can see well under water, but I cannot see distant objects clearly on land.

My sharp beak is great for catching fish.

When I swim, I draw my head back into my neck.

EYE, EYE

A penguin's eyes are protected by special see-through 'eyelids'. This stops the ice-cold, salty water from hurting the bird's eyes.

Let's go for a swim, Dad!

DID YOU KNOW?

SHARP BILLS

- A penguin uses its beak, or bill, to catch its food. Its mouth is lined with backward-pointing spines to help the penguin grip and swallow its wriggly dinner.
- Penguins clean and preen their feathers with their bill. The penguin spreads oil from its body over its feathers to keep them waterproof.
- A penguin gets rid of salt from its body through special parts of its bill. This means the penguin can drink sea water without becoming ill.

WHERE I LIVE

Penguins are found only in the southern part of the world. They live in many areas, from Antarctica to the coasts of New Zealand and South America. Some are even found in warmer waters near South Africa and the Galapagos Islands. Penguins spend most of their time at sea. They often only come ashore to moult and to lay their eggs.

SUPER SLIDERS

Emperor penguins slide or waddle over the ice to reach their breeding ground. If an emperor penguin wants to move quickly, it toboggans down icy slopes on its tummy. It's a speedy way to get around and looks fun, too!

NEW ZEALAND

Come on Priscilla, let's have a go!

WARM BURROWS

Magellanic penguins live in cold coastal waters around Chile and Argentina. They nest in deep burrows, where their chicks stay until they grow adult feathers.

SOUTH AMERICA

AFRICA

ANTARCTICA

·SOUTH POLE

TRALIA

That's where we live!

DID YOU KNOW?

ICY HOME

- In summer, the sun never sets in Antarctica. In winter, it's dark 24 hours a day.
- The lowest temperature on earth, −89°C, was taken at a research station in Antarctica.
- Antarctica is swept by violent gales that gust at up to 320 kilometres per hour.
- It's so cold in the Antarctic that if you dropped a metal bar, it would shatter like glass.

WHERE IN THE WORLD?

Emperor penguins live only on the Antarctic pack ice and in the surrounding ocean. Antarctica is a huge continent; it's almost twice the size of Australia. It is covered by ice and is the coldest place on earth. An emperor penguin's thick layer of blubber and windproof feathers help keep it warm in its icy home.

Antarctica is almost completely covered by a huge sheet of ice. Very little survives there except for a few plants and tiny insects. But the seas around Antarctica swarm with life. Masses of plankton and shrimp-like krill float in the water near the surface. These provide food for fish, squid, seals, seabirds and huge whales.

HUNGRY HUNTER

The sperm whale is the largest of the toothed whales. It grows up to 20 metres long and weighs about 55 tonnes – that's as much as ten elephants. Sperm whales have huge appetites. A sperm whale needs to gobble up lots of squid and fish to fill its tummy. The stomach of one sperm whale contained about 28,000 small squid!

He's a hungry hunter.

NOISY NOSE!

The male, or bull, elephant seal has a huge, trunk-like nose. He bellows to attract mates and warn other males to keep away. His big nose acts like a loudspeaker, so his calls carry a long way across the ice.

WIDE WINGS

The wandering albatross is a master flier. With a wingspan of over three metres, it has the longest wings of any living bird. It swoops and glides over the open Antarctic seas, searching for a tasty fish meal. It can travel over 800 kilometres per day and often stays at sea for months at a time.

Emperor penguins often live and swim together, but they usually hunt alone. They breed on the Antarctic pack ice in large groups called rookeries. Male and female emperor penguins usually pair for life. At breeding time they call and search for each other on the pack ice. Their calls can be heard a kilometre away.

We penguins are a friendly bunch. We like to 'talk' to one another. We each have our own special call so that we can tell each other apart. We also bow to greet each other when we meet!

Priscilla is going to be the most beautiful bird in the flock!

This is me, with Priscilla and her mum, Patsy. We're a very happy family. Patsy and I have been together three years and Priscilla is the third chick we've had.

I'm a good father to little Priscilla. We often play together while Patsy is hunting out at sea.

13

A female emperor penguin lays one egg between May and July, during the Antarctic winter. But emperor penguins do not build a nest. Instead, they carry the egg on top of their feet, covering it with their lower body. At first, Mum and Dad share the job. Then the female returns to the sea to feed. Dad looks after the egg on his own by covering it with a special flap of skin on his belly.

TOP DAD

The male penguin is a good dad. He keeps the egg warm on his feet for up to two months. During this time he does not eat. No wonder he loses half his body weight! The male penguins huddle together to keep warm.

I think it's starting to hatch!

14

Can I join your huddle to warm up?

BABY FILE

BIRTH

Dad incubates the egg for about 60 days. Then Mum usually takes over just before the egg hatches. The fluffy grey chick stays snug and safe on its mum's feet.

KEEPING WARM

A young penguin chick stays warm and snug beneath its mum's feathery tummy. Groups of penguins huddle together, taking turns to be on the edge.

SIX WEEKS

The chick grows quickly on the fishy meals 'sicked-up' by its parents. By six or seven weeks old it snuggles up with other chicks while Mum and Dad go fishing.

FOUR TO SIX MONTHS

The young penguins lose, or moult, their downy feathers and grow adult ones. It is now summer and the young penguins will soon go to sea to hunt by themselves.

15

Most birds spend little time on the ground, and fly away at the sight of a predator. However, there are some birds, like the penguin, that can't fly. Flightless birds have developed in remote areas or on islands where they have few enemies. Some flightless birds, like the ostrich, are huge and use speed to escape. Others, like the kiwi, hide away in the undergrowth.

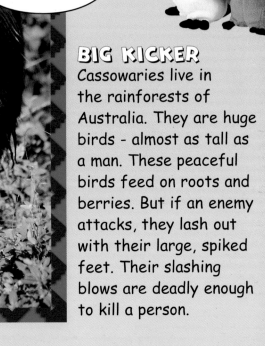

Keep close to me, Priscilla!

BIG KICKER

Cassowaries live in the rainforests of Australia. They are huge birds - almost as tall as a man. These peaceful birds feed on roots and berries. But if an enemy attacks, they lash out with their large, spiked feet. Their slashing blows are deadly enough to kill a person.

SHY BIRDS

Many birds in New Zealand, such as kiwis, can't fly. Until people arrived, about 1,000 years ago, no big predators lived there. So birds didn't need to fly to escape from their enemies. The shy kiwi hides by day and hunts at night. It sniffs out creepy-crawlies and pecks at them with its long beak.

RARE PARROT

The New Zealand kakapo, or owl parrot, is one of the rarest birds in the world. Kakapos can't fly, but they can run fast and glide. They climb to the tops of trees using their strong beaks and claws. Then they glide for about 100 metres.

17

WHAT I EAT

Penguins are hunters. They chase and catch fish, squid and shrimps. A penguin snaps up its prey with its sharp-tipped bill and swallows the fishy meal whole. In summer, penguins must gobble up as much food as possible to build up a thick layer of fat to keep them warm and nourished through the winter.

DARING DIVER

Unlike flying birds, penguins do not have light, air-filled bones. They have solid, heavy bones that make it easier for the penguin to dive deep into the icy ocean and stay under water.

DID YOU KNOW?

- Emperor penguins can dive to depths of 260 metres and stay under water for up to 20 minutes. That's far longer than any other bird.
- Sometimes penguins will travel up to 1,000 kilometres in search of food.

TEATIME!

Humboldt penguins live along the coast of Peru and Chile. They usually dig burrow-like nests among piles of seabird droppings, which form heaps in caves and along cliffs. These droppings are called guano. Humboldt penguins enjoy snacking on fish. They dive into the water and grab a tasty fish with their pointed beaks.

First to catch a fish wins!

HUNTER OR HUNTED?

Squid are also hunters. They glide silently through the water snaring prey in their long tentacles. If danger threatens, a squid can speed away by shooting out a jet of water. But squid are no match for a powerful penguin. It can swallow a small squid in one gulp!

NO FRIEND OF MINE!

An adult emperor penguin has few natural enemies on the Antarctic ice. The biggest killers are cold and starvation. But large seabirds often swoop down to the pack ice and snap up penguin chicks and eggs. There are many more predators in the sea. Seals, sea lions, sharks and killer whales all lie in wait to catch and eat unwary penguins.

COOL KILLERS

Killer whales, or orcas, are deadly predators. They will tip over an ice floe and gobble up the penguins resting on top.

DID YOU KNOW?

KILLER COLD

Sometimes a male penguin almost starves from lack of food while incubating his egg. If he gets too hungry, he may abandon his egg on the ice and return to the sea to feed. Then the egg will freeze and die.

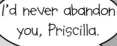

I'd never abandon you, Priscilla.

SEA LEOPARD

Leopard seals are fast-moving, hungry hunters with a mouthful of sharp teeth. They lie in wait at the water's edge, ready to seize penguins as they leap into the sea. One spotted leopard seal was found with 73 kilograms of penguin in its stomach. This is equivalent to two or three adult emperor penguins!

EGG THIEF

The giant petrel likes nothing better than a tasty meal of penguin eggs or chicks. It swoops down and attacks with its strong, sharp beak. Petrels can kill even fully-grown penguins.

21

A DAY IN MY LIFE

5:00 AM

The sun had risen! It was the first time after the long winter darkness. Soon it will be summer. Priscilla was fast asleep, snuggled up against me to keep warm.

8:00 AM

Priscilla was hungry and begged for food. I still had some left in my stomach, so I fed her.

9:00 AM

It was cold, but not too windy. I was very hungry. I decided to take Priscilla to the crèche and leave her there while I went fishing.

11:00 AM

I showed Priscilla how to slide along on her tummy. Tobogganing is a great way to get around! She called out to tell her friends she was coming.

12:00 NOON

Priscilla cuddled up with the other chicks. She will be warm and safe with Pete and Pam in charge. I slid off to a nearby hole in the ice to see if I could catch some tasty fish.

3:00 PM

I managed to catch quite a few silverfish. They were yummy! They didn't fill me up, but I was a bit less hungry. Patsy will be back soon, then I can go to sea for a good fish.

5:00 PM I arrived back at the crèche. Pete and Pam were very upset. Some giant petrels had attacked and snapped up three chicks. At least Priscilla was safe.

6:00 PM We tobogganed back to our patch on the ice. I gave Priscilla her fishy meal.

8:00 PM I preened my feathers and then settled down for a nap with my head under my flipper. Priscilla cuddled up close and had a snooze, too.

12:00 MIDNIGHT I woke with a start. I could hear Patsy calling across the ice. I called back to guide her to us.

2:00 AM Patsy arrived back home. We bowed and called to each other. Then she gave Priscilla a good feed. We cuddled up to sleep. The three of us will spend the night together, and then I will make my way to the sea in the morning.

5:00 AM Time for me to go. I bowed and called goodbye, and then set off. It will be a few weeks before I get back home again.

Perry

23

MY RELATIONS

Penguins probably developed from flying birds about 40 million years ago. Scientists think that some ancient penguins were almost as tall as a man! Today, there are about 17 different kinds, or species, of penguin. They all have fairly large heads, short necks and tubby, dark and white bodies. Penguins range in size from the tiny fairy penguin at 40 centimetres high, to the emperor penguin at over a metre tall.

CRESTED HOPPERS

Rockhopper penguins are quirky-looking birds. They have a yellow and black feathery crest, a bright orange-red bill and striking, red eyes. They're called 'rockhoppers' because they jump from rock to rock. They can even leap out of the sea onto the rocky coasts where they nest.

FAIRY PENGUIN

The fairy penguin is the smallest penguin species. These dark-blue penguins live around the coasts of New Zealand and southern Australia. After fishing all day, they scamper onto the beach and waddle back to their burrows.

NOISY TROOPS

Adelie penguins nest on islands in the Antarctic. Noisy troops of adelies waddle over 100 kilometres across the ice to reach their breeding grounds. Their journey can take over a week as each step they take only covers about 10 centimetres!

DID YOU KNOW?

All adult penguins have dark backs and light fronts. This helps them to blend in with the sea. The dark back blends in with the dark ocean when seen from above. And their pale front blends in with the lighter surface water when seen from below. This helps penguins hide from both their predators and their prey.

MAN AND ME

With their black and white coats and their comical walk, penguins are known and loved throughout the world. They are the heroes of many children's books and videos. They also star in lots of wildlife programmes and always draw a crowd in zoos.

COLD HOLIDAY

In recent years, tourists have taken trips to the Antarctic to watch penguins, seals and whales in the wild. But it's an icy holiday. Even in summer, it hardly ever gets above freezing. Your breath turns into a mist of tiny ice crystals. But the trip is worth it to see penguins at play. You might get really close to an emperor penguin, like this lucky photographer.

SCIENCE WATCH

No-one lives in Antarctica all the time. The only humans there are scientists, soldiers and tourists. Most of the time, the scientists live in cosy underground bases. They study the animals, oceans and weather. Many of the animals in Antarctica, such as the emperor penguin, are found nowhere else on earth.

Remember to smile for the camera!

POOR PENGUINS

- Early explorers killed penguins and salted the meat as food for their long sea journeys. Penguin blubber was used to make oil for lamps.
- Many people used to collect and eat penguin eggs. Collecting penguin eggs was stopped by law in 1969.
- Penguin feathers were once used for clothing, decoration and for stuffing mattresses.

WHAT DOES IT MEAN?

COMICAL
Something that is comical makes people laugh.

INCUBATE
To keep eggs warm so that they hatch into babies.

PACK ICE
Large pieces of floating ice crowded together in the sea.

ROOKERY
A colony of seabirds, such as penguins. A rookery is also the name for a colony of a type of bird called a rook.

RUFFLE
To make something less smooth. A penguin ruffles its feathers to break up the layer of air trapped next to its skin. This releases heat and cools the penguin down.

SHATTER
To break suddenly into tiny pieces.